GW01090570

HAPPINESS IS SHOOTING YOUR AGE

(The Joy and Despair of the Aged Golfer)

Newton Parks

Illustrations by

Addison Parks

Gardner Press, Inc.
6801 Lake Worth Road
Lake Worth, Florida 33467

ISBN # 0-89876-213-8

Library of Congress Cataloging in Publication Data

9 8 7 6 5 4 3 2

To that happy breed apart, the aging golfers in their eager pursuit of the elusive perfection ---or some faintly reasonable resemblance.

AUTHOR TO READER

Aging tycoons, and their lesser ilk, having mastered business, finance, plumbing, or whatever they spent most of their lives doing, expect to master golf. Redirecting their efforts from the demands of making a living to the comforts of a mere game should be easy.

It ain't necessarily so!

This booklet explains why. For the golfing geezer the obstacles are indeed high. But there is always the slight beam of hope that someday, somehow, somewhere, he (or you or I) will "shoot our age."

Adjust your bifocals and read on!

CONTENTS

CONTENTS (Continued)

1. HAPPINESS IS SHOOTING YOUR AGE

Every day across the land, aging retirees (bald heads hidden by weird hats) trudge about golf courses --- striving to "shoot their age."

The former scratch player stands a good chance: on reaching the age of seventy-plus, assuming he has taken care of himself and, God willing, he probably scores in the mid-seventies. One lovely day all his putts will drop and **he will have done it!!**

I fear the duffer will never make it. Normally he takes ninety-plus blows. In his seventies, there is no way that the required number of putts will go in. As the years move on, he is racing against time and, sadly, doomed to lose. He finds the yardage getting longer and the hole ever so small.

AGING RETIREES, BALD HEADS HIDDEN BY WEIRD HATS, TRUDGE ABOUT
GOLF COURSES

Does the ordinary, mid-handicapper (such as myself) have a rare chance? My handicap is fourteen with a strong following wind. That translates into scoring in the eighties with the occasional round in the high seventies. My age pushes the mid-seventies. Some day, perhaps, with all the breaks in my favor, and before complete decay sets in --------------

What is life without hope!

2. THE MATHEMATICS OF SHOOTING YOUR AGE

The fundamental problem is clearly demonstrated in the chart accompanying this page.

Skill (handicap) is shown plotted against age.

Assuming par is seventy-two, the rare person who shoots par every year of his life will, quite obviously, shoot his age at seventy-two.

On the other hand, as the chart clearly shows, the skill of the forty-year-old scratch golfer deteriorates with time. Theoretically he will shoot his age at seventy-six.

The duffer (defined by Webster's as an incompetent person whose handicap at age forty is twenty or over) has faint hope of shooting his age, according to the chart.

AGE VS GOLF SKILL (HANDICAP)

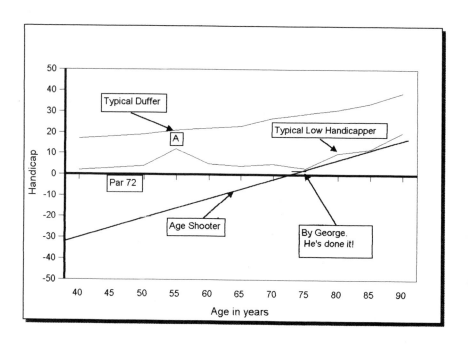

A - Upward Blip in handicap at age 55 due to nasty divorce with unduly harsh settlement.

For simplicity, chart assumes golfer always shoots his handicap

The enthusiastic and mathematically oriented reader may plot his own handicap and age through the years and discover when, if ever, he will shoot his age.

An army of golfers is on this quest. Of the 25 million enthusiasts in this country alone, over 3 million are seniors ---- that is, over sixty years old.

3. DEMOGRAPHICS FAVOR THE AGING GOLFER

Demographers tell us that in 1950 the probability of a sixty-five-year-old American reaching age ninety was only 7%. Forty years later it was 25%.

One can safely assume that golf, with all of its therapeutic advantages, will increase these percentages in favor of the aging golfer.

Laboratory studies on the longevity of Mediterranean fruit flies further support these aging trends.

Needless to say, all of this has a profound significance for the golfer struggling to shoot his age.

In the first place, it is apparent that he is going to have more years in which to fulfill his quest.

The previous chart that plotted age up to ninety is now obsolete and must be extended to one hundred. **(This is not as outrageous as it may first seem. A ninety-one-year-old lady at my club recently had a hole-in-one.)**

Secondly, if one is going to be around that much longer, the concept of middle-age must change. The golfer in his mid-seventies will now be middle-aged and will possess all the virility that this implies. A 200-yard drive will be expected and not generate a **"wow"** from his playing partner.

One other development affects this aging equation. It seems that traces of chromium in the human system increase longevity. The

MIDDLE-AGED AT 75---SINKING A PUTT.

trend to high-alloy golf clubs has obvious implications.

Some of the chromium will surely rub off!

4. THE BASICS OF GOLF

In any case, it is not an easy matter to "shoot one's age."

For one thing, the course is a reasonably long journey for an old guy.

From tee to green, an eighteen hole course is some four miles long as the crow flies.

This flight is entirely irrelevant **since hooks, slices, and shanks add another good half mile.**

To educate the uninitiated, par calls for stroking the small ball about seventy times over this substantial distance using a stick with a weight on the end.

The ball has to arrive safely at each hole on the long trip. Although the hole is four inches or so in diameter, it contracts as one gets older.

The ball itself has remained about the same size but has changed its color through the years.

Formerly white, it now comes in all the rainbow colors.

Unbelievably, one of my regular foursome, a sartorially resplendent senior, chooses a ball color each day to match his socks.

Color coordination has taken over from sanity. Senility is apparently setting in.

CHOOSING THE BALL COLOR TO MATCH SOCKS-----SENILITY?

5. WHY GOLFERS UNDERGO

ENJOYABLE TORTURE

Why do normally sensible, rational people subject themselves to this enjoyable anguish, golf-o-mania. Shakespeare sayeth: "There be some sports that are painful."

I suppose it is a replacement for their former careers.

They still crave:

      Competition

      Fellowship

      Risk and reward

      Joy and despair

      The attainable and

The unattainable

Displays of courage

Performance under pressure has always been par for their course.

By playing a game, they re-live their lives vicariously!!!

One never knows. Someday a silver-haired golfer you know may get the "new career" golf watch by shooting his age.

EMBARKING ON A NEW CAREER

6. MINI-HAPPINESS

Some 505 million rounds of golf were played last year in this country (National Golf Foundation).

Very few of these rounds ---- indeed, only 193 ---- were by seniors (or even juniors) who shot their age and were deliriously happy.

This is not to say that all the millions of remaining rounds were hapless. **There are degrees of happiness ---- mini or semi-happinesses.**

For example, some mini-happinesses are:

A booming drive

A crisp long-iron

A planned fade or draw

A delicate chip, well played

A hole-in-one (super-mini)

The plop sound of a long putt, or even a short one, settling

in the cup

Just plain participating (especially for seniors facing

sedentary alternatives)

All of the above are mini-happinesses compared to the sublimity

of shooting one's age. Senior Tour Pro, Joe Jiminez, tasted the

sublime by shooting his age at sixty-three (a tour record).

Mini-happinesses prevent happiness starvation on the golf course -

--- and enhance the aforementioned agelessness of golfers. **In**

what other sport do touring seniors display their substantial

talents for millions of eager fans?

The writer is presumptuous to discuss the sublimity of shooting

one's age, not having experienced it ---- as yet.

MINI-HAPPINESS----THE MELODIOUS SOUND OF A HOLED PUTT

7. AN OSCAR FOR THE GERIATRIC GOLFER

In the unlikely event that he will ever shoot his age, the senior golfer should know about the award, other than self-satisfaction, that awaits him.

The magazine *Golf Digest* devotes considerable attention to the age-shooter. First, it offers a certificate of accomplishment after proper credentials are submitted, meaning:

Personal data of age-shooter

An attested scorecard

A course over 6000 yards

The age-shooter also becomes a part of *Golf Digest*'s annual statistics. Extraordinary scores and multi-age shooting are recorded, as well.

Golf Digest keeps similar records on holes-in-one. **Since last year, there were 370,000 as compared with only 193 age shooters. The uniqueness of the skilled, senior golfer is worth serious attention.**

The astonishing wide disparity between the two accomplishments means one of two things:

> The self-effacing age-shooter does not admit to, or care to publicize, his feat since age, unfortunately, is not venerated in this country. In China, age shooters are knighted, made Mandarins, or better still, made War-Lords. (Ignoring Scotland, the Chinese National Golf Association, claims the game's origin in the third century B.C.)

Or, as is most likely, it is more difficult to shoot your age than to make a hole-in-one.

Last year, about 2.5 billion par-3 holes were played to produce the 370,000 holes-in-one. This roughly places the chances 1-in-7,000. In sharp contrast, only 193 of the 25 million golfers shot their age. (1 in about 125,000). The alert, numerate, skeptical and meticulous reader may challenge these comparisons, since a twenty-five-year-old golfer probably won't shoot a 25 and should not be considered in the calculation. In deference to youth, let's only count the 3 million seniors. Then we still have the formidable fact that only 1 in some 15,000 were age-shooters, clearly a much more exclusive club than one of holes-in-one. (This exclusivity does not pertain to professionals. **Miller Barber, the brilliant senior pro, is apt to shoot his age every third time he tees up.**)

Although the above figures apply to golf in America, they are probably also valid throughout the rest of the world where golf statistics are taken less seriously and not recorded as assiduously. Nonetheless, the *Royal & Ancient Golfer's Handbook*, that deals with a mass of worldwide golf matters, informs us (hold your hat!) that, in 1972, Arthur Thompson of Victoria, British Columbia shot his age at one hundred three.   He died two years later.... undoubtedly from post-game shock.   On the other extreme, at about the same time, Robert Klingaman was shooting his age as a childlike fifty-eight at Fayetteville, Pennsylvania.

Revel, you age-shooter. You are one of a rare breed. Stagger up and graciously accept your Oscar!!!

The Age-Shooter, a rare bird!

8. <u>LATE BLOOMERS</u>

A previous chart showed the deterioration of skill with aging. Although this is the norm, the contrary also occurs. Some golfers improve their game as they age. The reasons for this are clear. Younger players are distracted by:

Attractive, demanding wives

Child rearing

Making money

As time moves on, the golfer gets his values in order and gives golf its proper priority. Several things happen to assist the process:

His wife becomes addicted to bridge (or golf)

His children become self-sufficient (occasionally)

His business goes bankrupt

These matters all permit a golfer the time and clear-headedness to improve his game. Youthful brashness gives way to wisdom. Withered muscles hit shorter, but straighter, drives. A deft touch is acquired on and about the greens. A bad shot is brushed off with philosophical finesse. **Eventually, the senior golfer realizes he might shoot his age after all!**

The "late bloomer" phenomenon manifests itself in a number of ways:

> Club pros with unheard of names, such as Albus and Wargo, beat the likes of Nicklaus, Player and Palmer on the Senior Tour.

> Clyde Housel, a club player from Downey, California shot 16 strokes under his age at eighty-four.

> Last year, 20 golfers shot under their age 10 times.

Moral: Never give up. Keep trying!

A BLOOMING "LATE BLOOMER"

9. <u>PRISTINE FOR SOME, HELL FOR OTHERS</u>

The retired golfer has spent a good many years in:

Stuffy offices

Noisy factories

Crowded planes

And, perhaps, deep and dark mines

He now finds the golf course a welcome change.

The terrain often features rolling hills, bubbling brooks,

peaceful lakes and quiet woodlands.

Romantic bridges straddle the streams.

Birds chirp, ducks waddle, swans glide.

Sandy beaches (traps) dot the way.

Flora and fauna abound.

The pictorial beauty is arresting.

The spirit is lifted. The soul soars!

Moreover, the setting is so much more serene than at home, where one is apt to encounter a babbling mate.

Strangely, in spite of the pristine splendor, there are those who find the trees treacherous, the brooks a disaster and the beaches upsetting.

And, from time to time, the delightful calm is **shattered by violent oaths ---- worthy of the most ferocious drill sergeant.**

THE DELIGHTFUL CALM IS SHATTERED BY VIOLENT OATHS WORTHY OF
THE MOST FEROCIOUS DRILL SERGEANT

10. THE AGED GOLFER RESORTS TO HIGH TECH

In an effort to defy the laws of physics dealing with the impact of force on a stationary object (as well as the ruthless inevitability of age) the harried golfer has turned to high tech.

Metallurgists are sought out who spend sleepless nights developing space-age alloys for shafts and club heads. Shapes and sizes of putters outnumber heavenly bodies. Each year, a new model driver (more costly) appears on the first tee. Therapists are called upon **to restore minds of terrified players who, knees bruised and bloody from constant knocking, stand frozen over a three-foot putt.**

Dimpled balls are crafted to go farther and straighter.

Patient club pros, **neglecting elegant blondes with lovely legs,** develop special swings for ancient muscles that have lost both tone and memory.

Instruction books become "best sellers" assuring us that we will be the next Arnold Palmer.

But this is all wasted science, about as effective as a rain dance!

Father Time looks down on all this with a knowing and malicious smirk.

In all His wisdom, He knows that a rose is a rose is a rose, and **a hacker, is a hacker, is a hacker.**

PATIENT CLUB PROS, NEGLECTING ELEGANT BLONDES WITH LOVELY LEGS,
DEVELOP SWINGS FOR ANCIENT MUSCLES WITHOUT TONE OR MEMORY

11. <u>GOLF IS A RELENTLESS PURSUIT</u>

Yet, in our earnest quest to "shoot our age," nothing daunts us.

Neither the hot sun, nor sleet, nor high wind is an obstacle.

A rumor is circulating in misguided feminist circles that a particularly rabid player refused to attend his wife's funeral because it interfered with his morning foursome.

This is pure, utter rubbish!

The fact of the matter is that he had the ceremony delayed to the late afternoon to avoid conflict with his morning game.

Proper respect, after all, is called for.

It is a gentleman's game!

They say.

DECEASED WIFE IS HONORED AFTER THE MORNING FOURSOME

12. <u>GOLF COURSE DESIGN FOR THE AGED</u>

Through the years, golf and its courses have changed in deference to those on Social Security.

A good many clubs now have what they euphemistically call members' tees. These tees, in effect, shorten the course. They generously permit senior players to maintain their egos and reach par four greens in regulation **without wrenching their backs!**

Similarly, golf carts are a Godsend ---- adding some ten years to one's golf life. The carts, for better or worse, have practically made caddies obsolete, which is just as well, since rising fees were sending some players to the local welfare office.

The rough has also become more friendly ---- thanks to favorable settings on grass mowers.

These days, a ball in the rough may sit up nicely and, indeed, be preferable to a fairway lie.

Beyond that, winter rules with improved lies often prevail in non-wintry conditions. (Brits find this appalling.)

Mulligans on the first drive are normal.

Conceding putts, when you think about it, is civilized behavior (and helps the score).

All in all, the struggle to shoot one's age is getting lots of help in lots of ways.

13. BETTING WAYS OF THE

SOCIAL SECURITY GENERATION

Golf is a betting game, especially for the sixty-somethings.

That is not to say that players of this vintage have a particularly insightful perspective. Many an ex-tycoon's weekend is destroyed by the loss of a two-dollar Nassau. **The same loser, without a second thought, trades in his BMW because of a puncture!**

Bets come in all sizes and colors: greenies, presses, birdies, sandies, chippies and the ubiquitous Nassau, everyone's favorite bet. **Even a particularly pious, parish priest, deep in a Lenten fast, welcomes a nice little Nassau ---- on Good Friday.**

To cut betting losses, golfers plead for strokes. The first tee finds

EVEN A PIOUS PARISH PRIEST, DEEP· IN A LENTEN FAST, WELCOMES
A TWO-DOLLAR NASSAU---ON GOOD FRIDAY

ONCE PROUD, STRONG MAN PLEADING FOR STROKES

once-proud, strong men accepting strokes as though they deserved them. The basis for these strokes, the handicap system, is supposedly a great leveler that evens out everyone's game. Sheer fantasy! **Any system that fails to discount scores posted in a hailstorm with force nine gales is seriously flawed.**

Anyway, all the fuss about winning is absolutely senseless for a number of reasons:

First, winnings are diluted since any decent sort shares them (not losses) with his wife. All golfers are decent sorts.

Secondly, all winnings are fully taxable at top rates according to I.R.S. Code 74, Section D, Paragraph 3.

Regardless, Las Vegas betting ploys are distracting for craggy-faced purists who simply want to "shoot their age."

Money, more so than power, corrupts!

ANY HANDICAP SYSTEM IS FLAWED THAT FAILS TO DISCOUNT SCORES
POSTED IN A HAILSTORM WITH FORCE NINE GALES

The need to bet and to win is pervasive.   To paraphrase

George Orwell, "Golf is war without the shooting."

EX-TYCOON IN DISTRESS AFTER LOSING TWO-DOLLAR NASSAU

14. SURE-CURE FOR "THE YIPS"

Second only to prostate problems, **the worst affliction for autumnal golfers (those in late years) is "the yips."** Yuppies never yip. Nor do hippies.

For the poorly informed, "the yips" is a putting stroke that is not a stroke. Rather, it is a jerk or a jab. Either way, it is disastrous and invariably results in a missed putt. (A yip is the yelping sound made by a frightened puppy. It is the same sound the dinosaur golfer makes on missing a short putt.)

The only redeeming feature of "the yips" is that it results in the gentlemanly gesture of the conceded putt ---- **that patronizing**

gesture to a yip-ridden foe.

The sole consolation for the yipping golfer is that he is in good company. World class players have had the curse.

Only "the shank" and "the whiff" are higher hurdles to "shooting one's age."

Conventional wisdom offers two remedies for curing "the yips." **Both are wrong!!**

First, manufacturers develop a wide range of putter types: long shafts, croquet heads, offset blades, to name a few. Secondly, players develop a variety of putting styles: side-saddle, cross-handed, back-handed, etc.

WITHIN THE LEATHER?----ANOTHER YIP CURE

The simple reason these cures fail is that they all call for intense concentration on the putt. This is self-defeating, creating tension and the subsequent yip. **The only proven remedy is to think about something else other than the putt about to be missed.** This distraction can be achieved by affixing a picture on the putter head that redirects one's thought process.

Suggested pictures for different age groups are:

      Madonna ---- 60s

      Marilyn Monroe ---- 70s

      Greta Garbo ---- 80s

      Marlene Dietrich ---- 90s

There are other picture options depending on one's mood on any particular day. These include:

      Your mother-in-law

THE YIPLESS PUTTER AT WORK

Your ex-wife

Today's stock market quotes

The Lord's Prayer

The head of the putter is designed so that these various distracting pictures can be inserted at your discretion (patents applied for).

15. THE SENIOR GOLFER AS A DUDE

These days, aging golfers discard banker's gray or policeman blue and burst forth like blooming buds in early May. Bizarre shirts, slacks, socks and sweaters adorn the first tee. Everything is brightly coloured: dress, golf bags, tees, headcovers, umbrellas and balls, everything except the somber gray clubs..but their days are numbered. Expect pea-green shafts and baby-blue club heads next season! Tennis racquets have now gone that way.

No golf hat can rival for dash the "Marlboro man," Stetson, or the plantation straw. They liven an old codger's step and make the years recede just a bit...together with all threats of skin cancer.

Age-gap not withstanding, young pro Payne Stewart is the sartorial standard-bearer...making drab peasants of all opponents.

Peacock Payne of the NFL colour schemes, of the perky cap, of the smart knickers, puts to shame the stylish dandies of yesteryear: Walter Hagen, Jimmy Demaret and Doug Sanders.

In contrast to this bespoke splendor, some golfers, try as they may, are in constant disrepair. All seem rumpled, creased and stained...whether or not so...more at home toting beer kegs than club swinging. Their

bellies bulge

shirt-tails fly

trousers droop

faces flush

Even a cool sun brings forth rivers of sweat..drenching everything in sight, particularly armpits. Nasty, unkind partners pray they won't emerge from the woods or the deepest rough.

GOLF FASHION: SCRUFFY A TO HIGH-STYLE Z

In efforts to maintain minimum standards, golf clubs have initiated dress codes. Leotards, cut-off jeans, boxer shorts, and cycling suits have been banished. Bared chests (for all sexes) are frowned upon...particularly in cold climes. Walking shorts, although permitted, are not recommended for spindly legs or bony knees. Certain women should not wear slacks. Certain men should not wear shorts!

As with most things in life, senior golf fashions range from A to Z. Most of our gear, thankfully, falls somewhere in between.

16. THE GROOVED SWING ????????

As Professor Higgins reminds us:

A golfer's way of swinging absolutely classifies him.

The moment he swings, other golfers criticize him.

Some even despise him.

But to have a good swing is one thing. To repeat it is quite another. The bane of all golfers: young or old, .male or female, pro or duffer, is consistency, or rather the lack of. How many

Glorious drives are followed by a miserable second shot?

Spectacular rounds, well below one's handicap, are followed by a disastrous score?

A GOLFER'S WAY OF SWINGING ABSOLUTELY CLASSIFIES HIM.
THE MOMENT HE SWINGS, OTHER GOLFERS CRITICIZE HIM.

Emerging young stars fade into obscure oblivion?

Too many indeed. **Both life and golf can be so cruel!**

The problem is, of course, erratic play. Yet the path to success seems quite clear: the proper shoulder turn, staying behind the ball, clubhead square at impact, etc., etc.

Why can't these basics be followed, day by day, to provide an agreeable result?

The pat answer is loss of concentration. The golfer instead of thinking about the shot at hand, loses his train of thought and is distracted by other matters, i.e. Mongolian trade deficit.

Distractions are understandable but the excuse is not supportable, **particularly for senior golfers who tend to have short attention spans, and could be thinking of these issues for only a fraction of a second, not long enough to cause that lousy swing!**

Another, more plausible, reason for erratic play must be sought.

For the aging golfer, recall may be the culprit-----muscle recall. The arms, the back, the hands and the legs may just forget to act together each and every time. Alas--a dismal shot!!!

But, perhaps, the real answer has to do with male ego. Consistency, they say, is the handmaiden of small minds--- and if there is anything that repels the proud golfer, it is small mindedness. He looks with disdain at the idiot with a grooved, effortless swing----who confines his vacant day to the boredom of the fairway.

If consistency is the stuff of small minds, then most golfers are roaring intellectuals!!

IF CONSISTENCY IS THE STUFF OF SMALL MINDS, GOLFERS
ARE INTELLECTUALS!!!!!!!!!

17. THE GOLFER AS THE MUSIC MAN

Music and mathematics are closely linked; similarly, music and golf. Both have to do with tempo and rhythm. Approach Arnold Palmer on the practice tee, Ask him what he is working on. He will probably say, "My rhythm."

For the gerontic golfer, rhythm is of added importance. Smoothness must replace strength. An aged friend hums "The Blue Danube" between each shot. Yet, he never puts a ball in the water.

If you hum, pay attention to the tune. Neither rap nor ragtime is recommended for obvious reasons.

I've got rhythm!
On green fairways.
Who could ask for anything more?

Nocturnes tend to be lulling---bad for the concentration.

Dirges are too funereal---anathema for the aging golfer.

Waltzes and serenades are perfect, as well as ballads. In fact, hum anything that Perry Como used to sing and it should help your swing. He was, and still is, a first class golfer. **A strong vote for rhythm.**

Social scientists have discovered that listening to music (Mozart in particular) improves the mind---for short intervals. Since golf is a mental game, a movement is afoot to wire golf courses for stereo. This will take time. While you wait, keep humming.

Another analogy relating to music and golf is the longevity of the participants. Both musicians and golfers seem to go on indefinitely. Hogan, Nelson and Sarazen immediately come to mind. Stokowski, Horowitz and Rubenstein are but a few of many musicians who played well into the twilight years. Then there is Bob Hope who started as a song and dance man and recently had a hole in one (in his early nineties!).

The secret is that golf and music are both physical and cerebral in their own way.

Doddering to either the tee or the podium keeps the body and the mind alive with rhythmic movement.

18. THE LADIES, GOD BLESS 'EM

This book may appear to ignore the lady golfer (25% of all seniors).

Not so!!

Now, near the close of the 20th century, an array of gracious and graceful ladies adorn most golf courses at most hours of the day. It wasn't always so! These days, even that splendid bastion of male isolation, the Augusta National Golf Club, permits ladies ---- **as guests**.

But this book is about aged or aging golfers.

Not that ladies don't age, but they are more discreet about it.

LADY OF DUBIOUS YEARS, "SHOOTING HER AGE"

The process is more elusive. It is a sensitive subject.

That is their well-deserved privilege. We honor it.

Nonetheless, they still strive to "shoot their age."

However, on that fateful day, they alone will know!!!!!!!!!!!!!!!

In fact, only four ladies are on record (<u>Golf Digest</u>) as having shot their age.

Astonishingly, Rose Montgomery of Palm Springs, California scored a 92 at age ninety-six.

Match that, macho male!

19. A GOLF PILGRIMAGE

'Think you've mastered the game?

'Think your swing is grooved?

'Think you're about to shoot your age?!

Come down from that high horse. Take a golf pilgrimage to Scotland, "the cradle of the game." Have an exhilarating, but humbling, experience. Be forewarned, however, your handicap will suffer.

Need one say, golf in Scotland is a formidable challenge for the aging golfer (or any golfer).

Fierce winds blow in from the North or Irish Seas.

Greens are hard and don't hold.

Preferred lies are unthinkable.

Tall Scots whose shots go astray find themselves in heather up to their navel. Short Scots, in a similar plight, are lost for hours.

Drizzling, cold rains are normal. Full-lipped bunkers are the envy of female pop stars.

Off-setting these considerable perils is the rarest jewel in Scotland's crown, the famed and weathered Scot caddie in his uniform of rumpled suit, battered tie, and faded cap. But appearances are deceptive. For a modest fee, he

Totes your bag

Restructures your swing

Corrects your grip

SHORT SCOT LOST IN HIGH HEATHER

Reads the greens

Selects your club

Ignores your failures

Maintains your moral

Lauds your faintest efforts

Beyond this, at the end of the day, he will have straightened out your personal life! All are rendered with good humor, courtesy and respect.

As soccer is to Brazil and horse racing to Kentucky, golf is to Scotland. All classes, ages and sexes join in. They play it, watch it, talk it, revere it. Not too long ago, more courses were within a 25-mile radius of Glasgow than on the entire European continent.

The Scottish zeal for the game is limitless, or beyond. At St. Andrews, a certain lady had tee rights to six starting times a day on the Old Course for herself and guests.

The rights had been in her family for a hundred years, **and were recently sold to the St. Andrews Trust for $375,000. Her hardly befitting name was Gladys Cheape. But Scots know value when they see it!**

Golf historians place a crude version of the game in Scotland as far back as the twelfth century. The first club was established at Leith before our Revolution in 1764. The illustrious Royal and Ancient Golf Club of St. Andrews was formed in 1834, with King William IV named as patron, shortly thereafter. Little wonder it is sacred ground, shrouded with quiet tradition.

There is no mystery as to why the Scot golfer is so durable. Most walk the course either carrying his bag or pulling it by trolley. The weather is bracing to say the least. Golf and strong Scotch whiskey cure most ills and prolong the years.

On your pilgrimage you will do well to develop a wee

Scottish mood in anticipation of the experience. But leave

your bagpipes at home ---- too cumbersome for a 747. In

their place, some reading material is in order to shorten the

long flight and set the journey's tone. Bring along John

Updyke's classic short story, "Farrell's Caddy." It captures

the essence of Scottish golf. You'll arrive in Scotland

inspired, hopeful and salivating for the first tee. With luck,

you may even get Farrell's Sandy to carry your bag ---- and

preserve your ego.

Conquer the rigors of Scottish golf; feast on its

pleasantries; and return to America to shoot your age ----

readily!

20. SARAZEN, THE ELITE OF THE ELITE

Every golfer, particularly those "long in the tooth," needs a hero, someone inspirational who will guide him on his long quest to be an age-shooter. He especially needs a hero when having one of those days mom warned about. When

Long irons are short

Short irons are long

Drives dribble

Putts linger on the lip

Abandon all thoughts of suicide. Don't recycle those costly, high-tech clubs into a spacecraft. Rather, turn to your hero. What would he do?

If you don't have a golf hero, may I nominate Gene Sarazen? The golf world has a number of legendary figures but, to my mind, Sarazen is the elite of the elite. Let's look at the record:

A humble background, starting as a caddie, then a gofer in a pro shop.

U.S. Open Champion in 1932.

Masters Champion in 1935, thanks, in part, to a spectacular double-eagle on the par 5 fifteenth.

The first player to accomplish The Grand Slam (British Open, U.S. Open, PGA and Masters).

Made the 36 hole cut at the Masters at age sixty-one.

Age-shooter at sixty-nine.

Shot 75 on eve of being eighty.

A brief word about The British Open win. Sarazen had a regular English caddie, Daniels, who, by 1935, was sickly and old for a caddie (sixty-five). Nonetheless, Sarazen stayed with him. Together they won. Daniels died two months later ---- fulfilled.

GENE SARAZEN: A SENIOR SUPER HERO

Now in his nineties, Sarazen still plays relatively awesome golf, still in his "trademark knickers, still with the Cheshire Cat smile. Built close to the earth, only about 5'6", but his heart and spirit are on the high ground, up with the angels.

Keep Sarazen, your new hero, in mind when next faced with a tough putt!

21. THE GOLFER AS A POLITICAL FORCE

These days minorities, of all sorts, bask brightly in the political sun. It's time golfers come out of the shadows. Some 25 million strong, the golfing world is no small potatoes by any measure. **Its political clout** is enhanced by a distinguished membership. Going back to Ike, every President (except Carter) has been a golfer, more or less – usually less.

The aging golfer has two choices: either stay with his younger golfing brethren and become a part of a *morale majority;* or secede to the AARP and inherit a Washington lobby second to none, the envy of every minority group. Since senior golfers are short off the tee but long on integrity (as well as in the tooth), the choice is clear.

Kinship is a compelling factor with most minorities. But, granted that golf is addictive, the addiction doesn't seem to be genetic. **DNA blood samples taken from bleeding ulcers of notoriously poor putters show zero correlation.** Nonetheless, although not blood relatives, golfers love the game with equal passion.

The golfer bloc will have a strong political agenda:

Death to all animal species, endangered or not, that defecate on fairways.

The Greening of the desert.

Water conservation, except for parched golf courses

No deforestation, except for trees obstructing ball flight.

Zero taxes for clubs and players. Treasury revenue loss is more than offset by reduced health-care costs for serene, virile, long-lived golfers.

Move over Ross Perot. Arnie's army is on the move —— Charge!!!

STAND ASIDE, ROSS PEROT.

ARNIE'S ARMY IS ON THE MARCH!!!

22. QU'EST-CE QUE C'EST LE BONHEUR?

Light years ago, my daughter went to school in French Switzerland.

The last provocative theme they asked her to write was "Qu'est-ce que c'est le bonheur?" (What is happiness?)

Nowadays, when my French Canadian granddaughter asks me, "Grandpère, dites-moi, qu'est-ce que c'est le bonheur?"

Without hesitation, I reply **"To shoot my age, ma petite chérie."**

GRANDPERE, QU'EST—CE QUE C'EST LE BONHEUR

EPILOGUE

As of the date of publication, the author has yet to shoot his age.

Recently, he was about to see the promised land. Only a two-foot putt on the eighteenth green obstructed the view.

He yipped!

Ah, yes, the indignities of age---and the frailties.

Nonetheless, undismayed, the quest continues!

Is it the impossible dream, the unreachable star?

May the twilight linger longer!

THE QUEST CONTINUES!!!MAY THE TWILIGHT LINGER LONGER